| DATE DUE | | | |
|---|---|---|---|
| JAN 14 '76 | JUN 20 1979 | NOV 1 2 1980 | OCT 9 |
| MAR 5 '76 | JUL 1 1 1979 | MAR 2 1 1981 | 1988 |
| MAY 27 '76 | JUL 27 1979 | JUL 1 0 1984 | NOV 1 5 1988 |
| JUN 10 '76 | AUG 9 1979 | SEP 4 1984 | JUN 2 7 1988 |
| JUN 22 '76 | OCT 1 3 1979 | JUN 2 0 1984 | SEP 29 1988 |
| JUL 2 '76 | MAR 3 1 1979 | JUL 1 0 1986 | MAY 8 1991 |
| JUL 8 '76 | AUG 7 1979 | AUG 1 5 1988 | |
| JUL 2 4 '76 | FEB 1 9 1980 | AUG 3 0 | JUN 2 1 1991 |
| JUN 1 1 '77 | JUN 1 7 1980 | JUN 2 7 1989 | |
| AUG 1 2 | JUL 2 3 1980 | | DEC 1 8 1991 |
| FEB 2 1 '78 | AUG 5 1980 | JUL 2 7 1989 | MAR 1 8 1992 |
| ASSOCIATED | AUG 2 5 1980 | AUG 1 4 1989 | JUN 8 1993 |

July 8

J
796.357  Hasegawa, Sam
Has      Mickey Mantle

superstars!
superstars!
superstars!
CREATIVE EDUCATION SPORTS SUPERSTARS

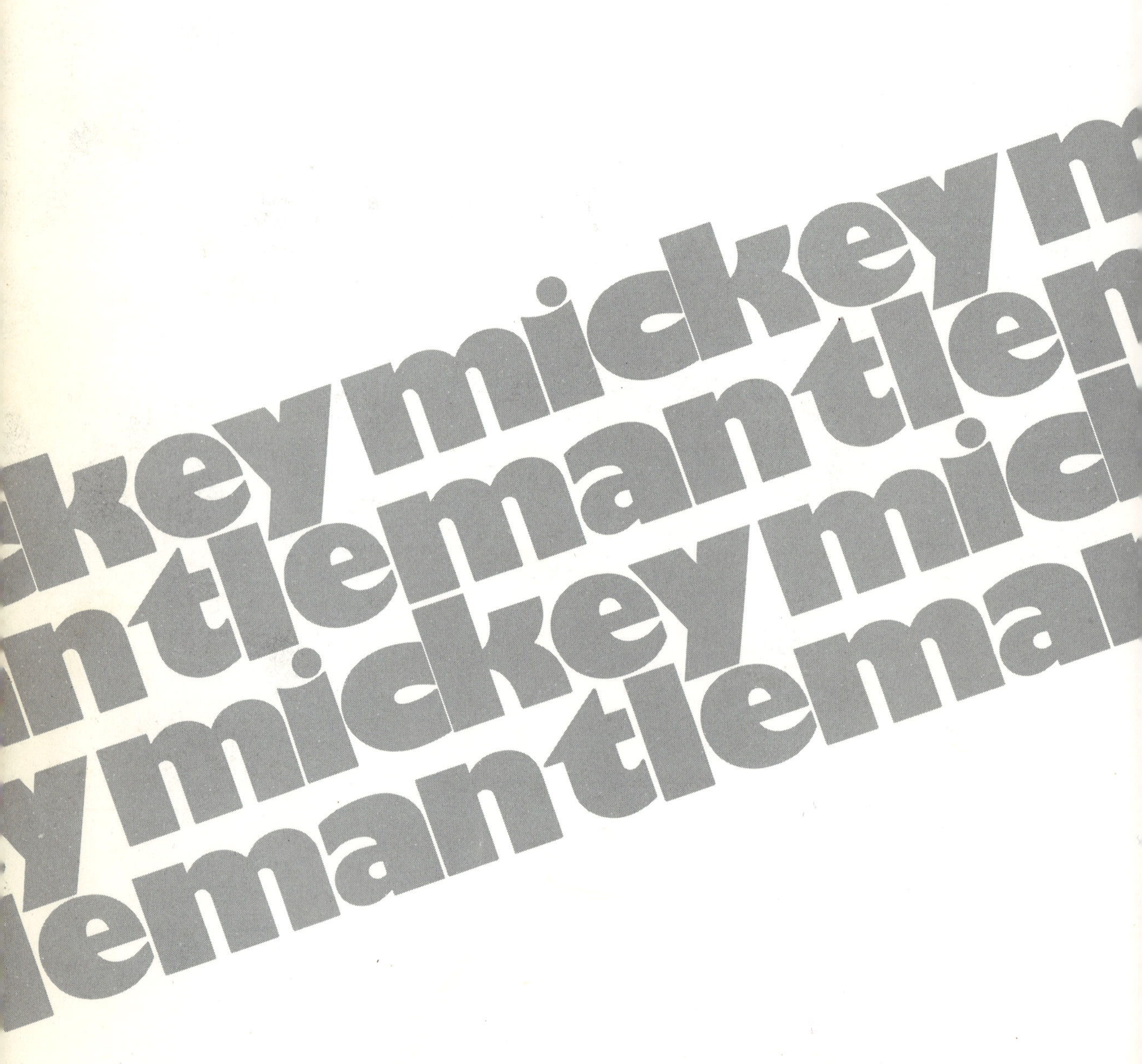

mickey mantle
mickey mantle
mickey mantle
mickey mantle

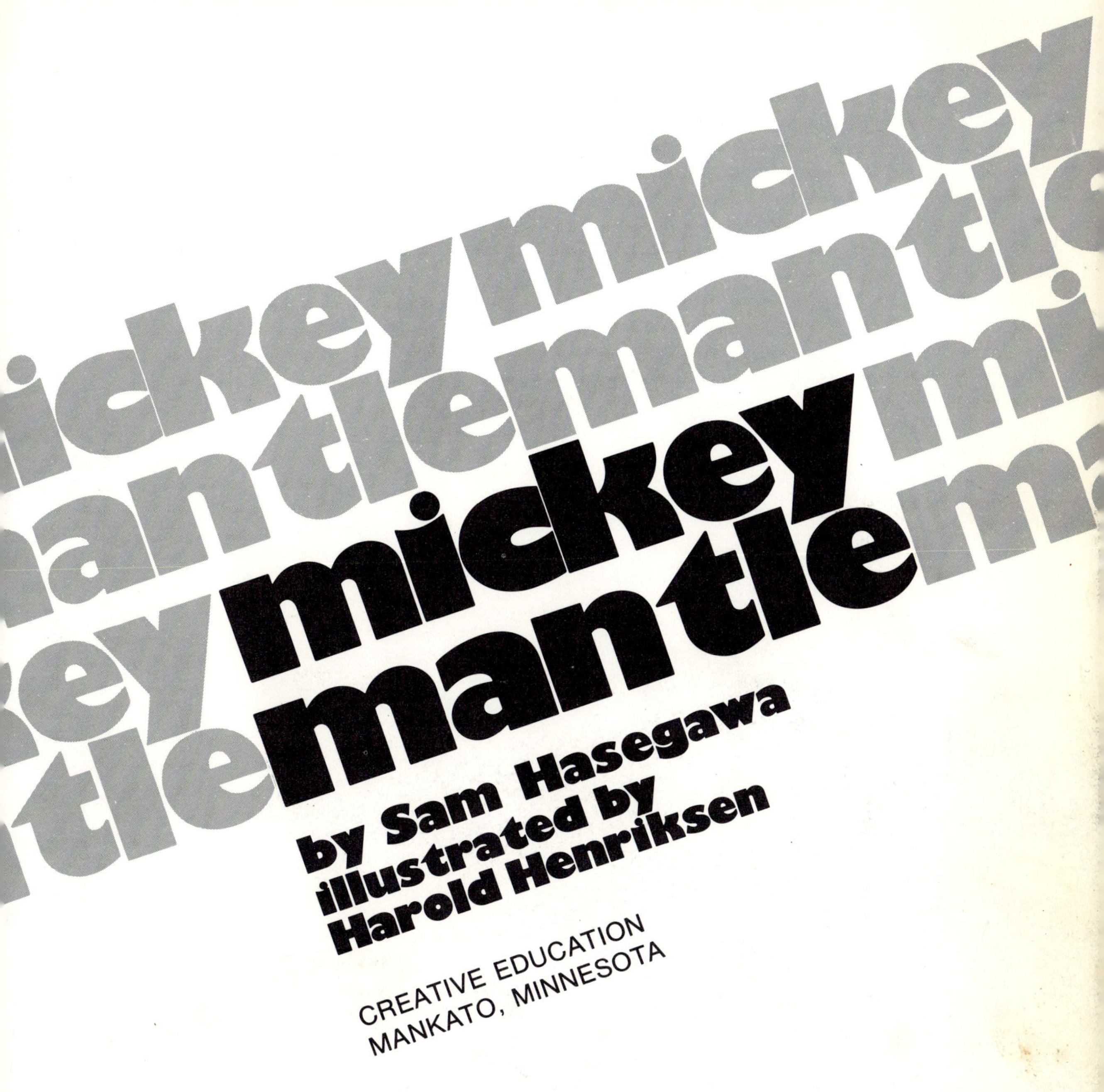


# mickey mantle

by Sam Hasegawa

illustrated by
Harold Henriksen

CREATIVE EDUCATION
MANKATO, MINNESOTA

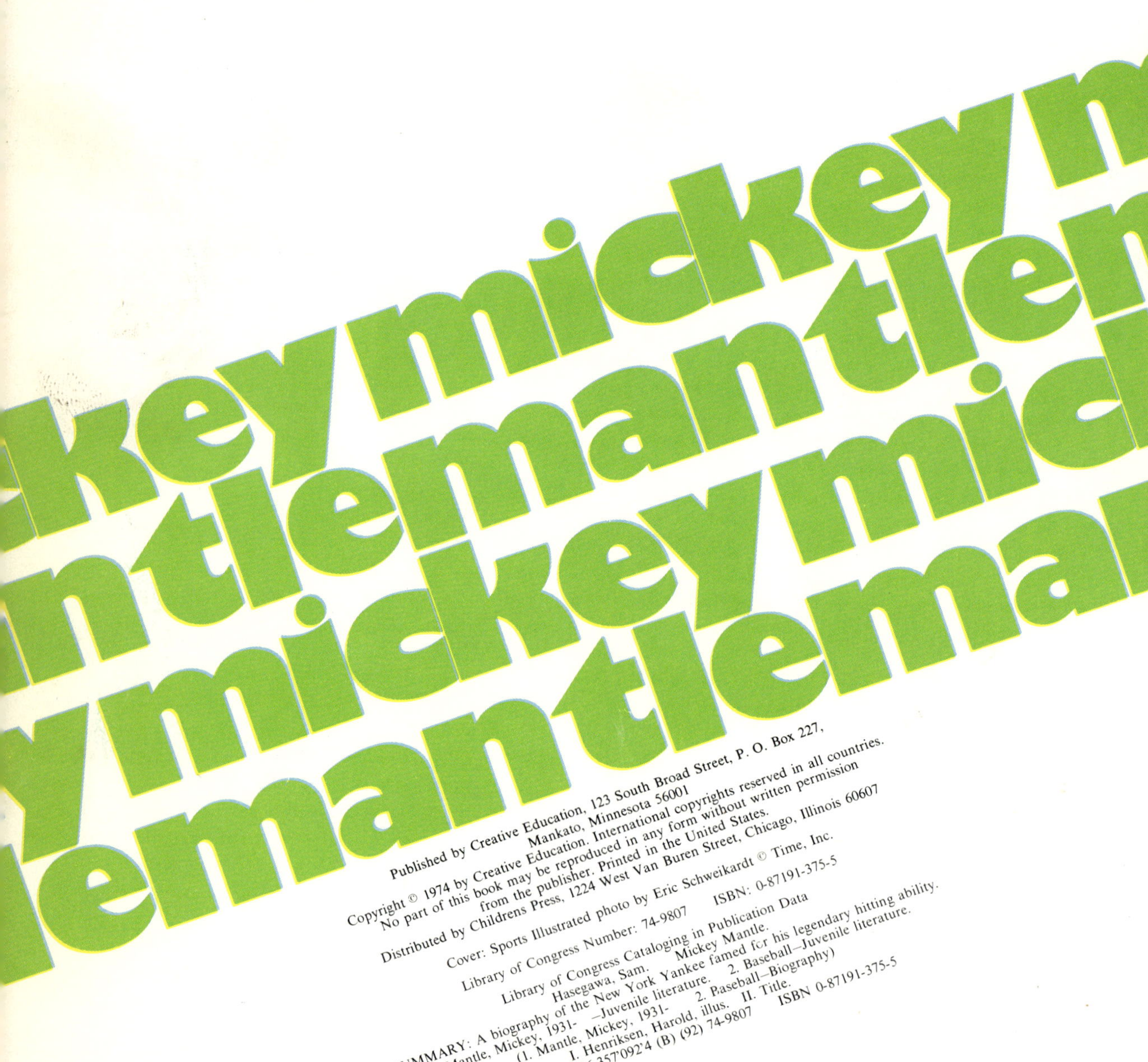



Published by Creative Education, 123 South Broad Street, P. O. Box 227, Mankato, Minnesota 56001

Copyright © 1974 by Creative Education. International copyrights reserved in all countries. No part of this book may be reproduced in any form without written permission from the publisher. Printed in the United States.

Distributed by Childrens Press, 1224 West Van Buren Street, Chicago, Illinois 60607

Cover: Sports Illustrated photo by Eric Schweikardt © Time, Inc.

Library of Congress Number: 74-9807     ISBN: 0-87191-375-5

Library of Congress Cataloging in Publication Data
Hasegawa, Sam.     Mickey Mantle.
SUMMARY: A biography of the New York Yankee famed for his legendary hitting ability.
I. Mantle, Mickey, 1931-     —Juvenile literature.
(1. Mantle, Mickey, 1931-     2. Baseball—Juvenile literature.
2. Baseball—Biography)
I. Henriksen, Harold, illus.     II. Title.
GV865.M33H37  796.357'092'4 (B) (92) 74-9807     ISBN 0-87191-375-5

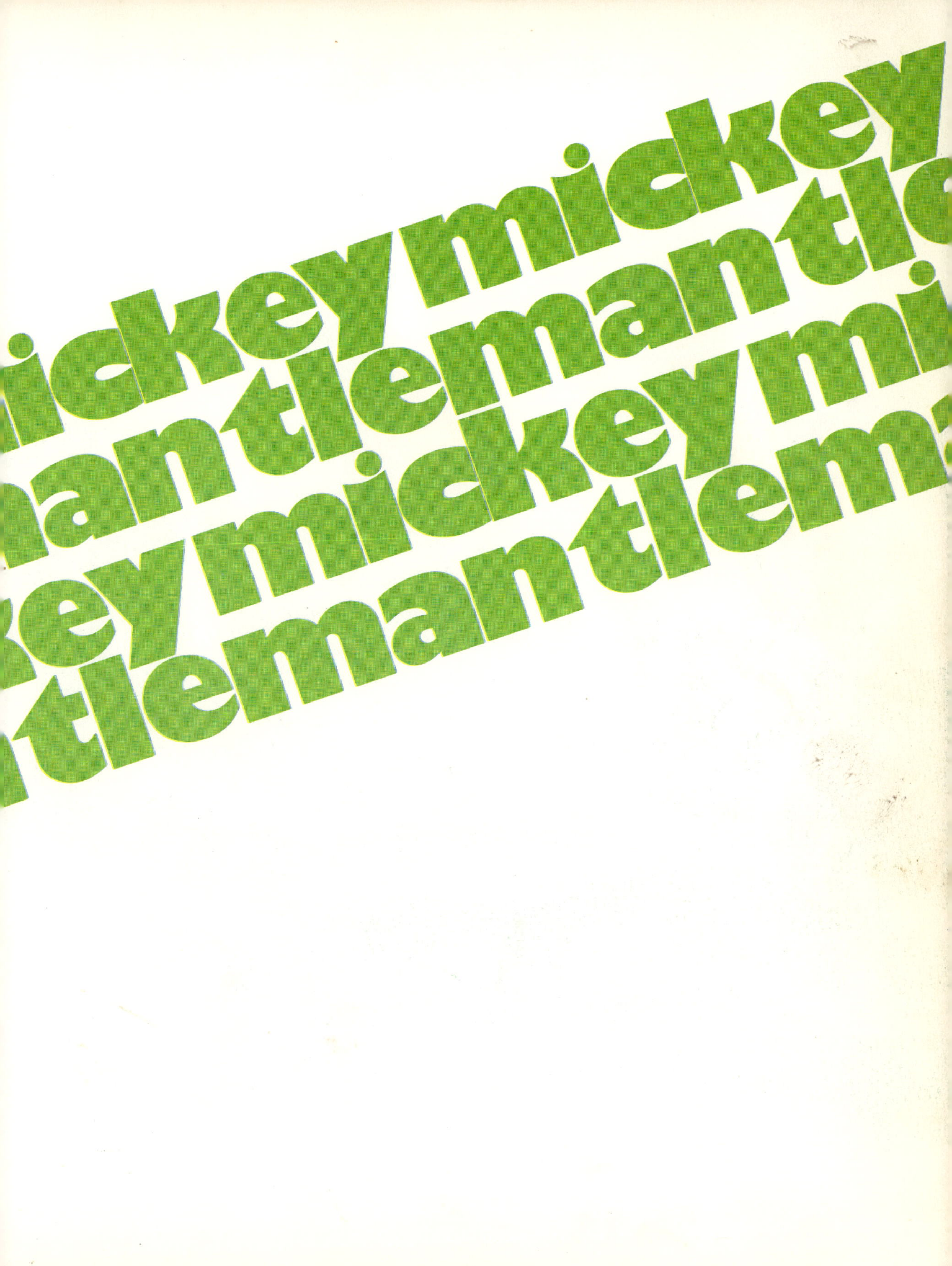

It was a sultry summer morning. The brilliant glare of the sun seemed to have washed the color from the cloudless sky. The blue appeared faded, almost white.

Gusts of hot wind kicked up clouds of dust from the dirt field. There in the brightness and swirling dust, Mickey Mantle and two friends were playing baseball.

Commerce, Oklahoma, is a small mining town; and the field had once been a mining site. You could see the old abandoned mine shafts and the slag heaps. The fenced-off holes were places where cave-ins had occurred.

The neighborhood kids called the field the Alkali—maybe because it was so dry and dusty, like an alkali desert.

Under the fierce light of the summer sun, it did seem to be a little desert. There was scarcely a single blade of grass, and the ground was baked hard as concrete.

Mickey and his friends came here almost every day to play ball. They played a simple game. One pitched, one batted and one took the field. After 3 outs they changed positions.

Each pretended to be his favorite major league team. Mickey always chose to be the New York Yankees. He knew the players and the batting order. Each time at bat Mickey would go through the line-up, becoming one player and then another. He even batted right-handed or left-handed according to the way each player hit.

Mickey inherited the love of baseball and the dream of becoming a pro from his father. Elven Mantle had once been a semi-professional player. More than anything else, he had wanted to make the big leagues; but he had never had the talent. He had ended up working in the mines.

Almost from the moment of his first son's birth, Elven hoped the boy would become a baseball player. He named the child Mickey, after Mickey Cochrane, the great catcher. Cochrane was Elven's personal baseball hero.

Elven spent a lot of time teaching his young son the fundamentals of the game. Nearly every spring and summer afternoon was devoted to workouts. Father and son would practice together, playing pepper.

It was Elven who taught Mickey to switch-hit. Mickey was naturally a right-hander. Batting left-handed was at first uncomfortable for him. But his father kept after him, making him practice hitting both ways. Elven also insisted that, in any game, Mickey always bat left-handed against a right-handed pitcher.

The combination of Mickey's natural ability and his father's coaching produced rapid results. The summer after high school graduation in 1949, Mickey signed a contract with the Yankee organization.

In the spring of 1951, Mickey was asked to come to the Yankees' spring training camp in Phoenix, Arizona. It almost seemed that Mickey's childhood dream had just changed locations—from the arid Alkali to the Arizona desert.

Mickey was only 19. He had less than 2 years of minor league ball behind him. Understandably, few people were aware of what he could do. It was not long, however, before everyone was talking about him.

No one had ever seen anyone hit quite the way Mickey did. In batting practice he would often hit 4 or 5 balls in a row over the fence. That was batting right-handed.

Then he would switch to the other side of the plate and duplicate the feat.

It was not just Mickey's tremendous power from either side of the plate that was amazing. No player in camp came close to matching his running speed. In the opinion of Yankee coach, Bill Dickey, Mickey was the fastest man ever to step onto a ball field.

Joe DiMaggio, one of the best players of all time, called Mickey the greatest rookie he had ever seen.

By the end of spring training, the press was heralding Mickey as the next Yankee superstar. They called him the successor to Ruth, Gehrig, and DiMaggio.

Mickey more than lived up to his publicity during the exhibition season. His .402 batting average was the highest on the team, and he led the Yankees in home runs. In several parks he hit homers of record length.

Still, at the close of exhibition season, Mickey, and many other people, thought that he would be sent back to the minors.

Mickey's lack of experience was one reason. The previous season, he had played with a Class C team, 4 leagues below the majors.

Furthermore, Mickey had always been a shortstop. Casey Stengel, the Yankee manager, had had Mickey playing in right field. Before that spring, Mickey had never played the outfield at all.

However, Mickey's performance had been so incredible that the Yankees wanted his bat in the line-up right away. When the team took the field for the season opener, Mickey was in right field, next to his boyhood hero, Joe DiMaggio.

For Mickey, it had all happened so fast that it seemed unreal. Almost overnight his life-long dream had become fact.

But as the season went on, the dream began to take on a nightmarish quality.

Pitchers began to discover Mickey's weaknesses as a batter. His hitting started to fall off. The harder he tried, the worse it seemed to get. In desperation he began to swing wildly, going after pitches way out of the strike zone.

The number of strikeouts climbed throughout July. Each one added to Mickey's frustration a little more. Finally, in a doubleheader at Boston, Mickey struck out 5 times in a row. When he returned to the bench after the fifth one, he could not hold back the tears.

After the game Mickey found out that he would be sent back to the minors. He was to join the Kansas City club, a Class AAA team.

NEW YO
NEW YORK

STRIKE
STRIKE
STRIKE
STRIKE
STRIKE

Mickey felt that he had blown his chance to make it in the majors. He had done well in the pre-season. Still, he had not hit big league pitching consistently in regular season play—when it really counted.

The strikeouts continued with frustrating regularity after Mickey joined the Kansas City team, which was on a road trip. When the trip came to an end, Mickey had gone hitless in 22 consecutive times at bat.

During the train ride back to Kansas City, Mickey's mind was full of painful thoughts. He had tried, harder than ever before in his life. Still, he thought, he had failed miserably. He began to think that the pre-season must have been a fluke. In the midst of thoughts like these, memories of home and of his father began to drift through his mind. The warm images of life in Commerce were a comforting contrast to the torment of the past few weeks.

Mickey felt sure his dad would understand how he felt. Elven Mantle had once known the same bitter disappointment himself.

Mickey decided to call home. At the next stop-over he telephoned his dad and asked him to come to Kansas City to pick him up at the station. Mickey said that he wanted to go home.

When Mickey stepped off the train in Kansas City,

he saw his dad waiting on the platform. All the feelings that had been dammed up inside of him rushed to the surface. Tears stung in his eyes.

Before they were out of the station, Mickey began to sob out his story. But the look on his father's face, cold and unsympathetic, stopped him short in mid-sentence. Mickey did not understand. In his confusion, he was unable to utter another word.

His father broke the silence. In a voice as icy as his expression, he said, "If that's how you're going to take it, you don't belong in the majors. If you don't have the guts to stick it out, then go ahead and quit. You can come home and work in the mines, like me, for the rest of your life."

Mickey was stunned. But as the feeling of hurt and shock wore away, he began to see himself in a different light. He suddenly saw himself as a small child, ready to quit after one failure. Instead of wanting to try all the harder, he had just given up. Then he had run to his father, expecting sympathy.

His father's words had jolted him to a new awareness. Mickey did not go home that day. Instead, he and his father went to the Kansas City ball park. In the game that evening Mickey played like a different person. With

1 2 3 4 5 6 7 8 9 10 10 H E
GIANTS 0 0 0 0 0 1 1
YANKS 1 1 0 0 2 4 0
AT BAT
BALL

his dad cheering from the stands, he smashed 2 homers. The slump was broken.

That day was a turning point. In the following weeks Mickey hit at a torrid pace. By August he had raised his average to .360 and had driven in 50 runs. This was what the Yankees had been waiting for. They recalled Mickey immediately.

That September the Mantles came to New York to see their son play in his first World Series. In the second game Mickey got his first Series hit. He surprised the other team with a bunt. Later, he scored.

Before he got another chance at the plate, he ran into bad luck. He was chasing a ball hit to right center when suddenly he crashed to the ground. It looked as though he had been shot. He lay motionless while a stretcher was brought out to take him off the field.

Mickey, running at top speed, had caught his spikes on one of the wooden drain covers in the outfield grass. The fall had severely wrenched the cartilage in his right knee. He was through for the Series.

He could not have known that a greater shock awaited him at the hospital. His dad rode there with him. When they got out of the cab, Mickey put his arm around his father's shoulders to support himself. Without a word of warning, his dad collapsed under the weight. The two fell to the pavement.

That day Mickey learned that his dad had cancer. Elven had known for some time but had kept the news from Mickey. He had not wanted to allow anything to distract his son in his first shot at the major leagues.

The disease was in an advanced stage. Elven had to be hospitalized immediately. Father and son, lying in bed in the same room, watched the rest of the Series on TV.

Elven never did get to see Mickey attain stardom, but he had seen him make it to the big leagues. That winter he was part of another big event in his son's life. Mickey married Merlyn Johnson, his girl friend since high school, in December. In May, 1952, Elven Mantle died.

For the next several years Mickey struggled to fulfill the promise he had shown in the spring of 1951. He continued to be plagued by strikeouts, and his home run production was disappointingly low.

Part of the problem was the pressure Mickey played under. It was not enough for him to be good—people expected him to be great. Very few of them took into account his youth and lack of experience. Not many fans thought of the adjustment problems of a shy, small-town boy facing life in New York City and national publicity.

And then there were the inevitable comparisons with DiMaggio. The press had built Mickey up to be the successor to Joe, if not his superior.

When Mickey took over center field after DiMaggio's retirement, the fans expected him to perform as the veteran had. He was supposed to become a superstar overnight. When he did not, he became the target of some vicious booing.

Mickey had a greater problem—his own temper. All it took to trigger it was a few bad days at the plate. Then, every strikeout would be followed by violent swearing. Back in the dugout, he would take out his anger on the water cooler. It was dented in from the countless kicks and blows he had aimed at it. When he was really mad, Mickey had the habit of throwing bats—until the day a Mantle bat narrowly missed the leg of Yogi Berra, the Yankee catcher.

Once Mickey started to brood on his failings, he made needless errors. His temper ruined his concentration. But as the season went by, Mickey began to grow out of this phase. In 1956, in spring training camp, there was talk of a new Mantle.

Mickey did seem to be a different person. He was more self-assured, more relaxed, more talkative. He no

longer seemed the painfully shy country boy. The fits of anger grew rarer, the number of strikeouts fewer. More relaxed at the plate, he waited for his pitch.

The new-found confidence worked wonders. In the first month of the season Mickey hit 16 homers. By mid-season he was 17 games ahead of the pace Babe Ruth had set in his 60-home-run year.

As the season drew to a close, even the White House was following Mickey's progress. President Eisenhower came to a Yankees' game and asked Mickey to hit one for him. In his last at bat, Mickey did.

Mickey was in head-to-head competition with Ted Williams for the league batting championship. The outcome was uncertain until the final week, but Mickey's .353 average won it. Although he never did catch Ruth, his league leading totals of 52 homers and 130 RBIs made him the seventh man in history to win the Triple Crown. Mickey also topped the league in runs scored, total bases, and slugging percentage.

Because of his marvelous performance, Mickey became the unanimous choice for Most Valuable Player (MVP) in the American League.

The next season Mickey hit .365, his highest major league average. He belted 34 homers and led the league again in runs scored. For the role he played in leading the Yankees to yet another pennant, he was again voted MVP.

It seemed that everything had begun to go Mickey's way—until the World Series. In the third game, Mickey's first Series' luck repeated itself.

Mickey was on second, taking a good lead. He saw that the pitcher was going to throw to second, rather than to the plate. He dived for the bag, his right arm outstretched. The throw was wild. Red Schoendienst, the second baseman, lunged for the ball and came down on Mickey. Mickey's right shoulder took the full shock of Schoendienst's weight.

By that evening Mickey could not even swing a bat. Again, he was out for the rest of the Series. Without him, the Yankees lost.

The injury left Mickey with a chronic sore arm. He had once had one of the strongest arms in baseball. Once he had thrown a runner out at home from deep center field, over 250 feet away. The throw had been a perfect strike. The incredible thing was that Mickey, in a hurry to get the ball off, had thrown underhanded.

He would never make throws like that again. His batting, already affected by the bad knee, would also suffer.

The next season, the shoulder still bothering him, Mickey's average dropped 61 points. He still hit 42 homers, enough to lead the league. But there was an ominous sign. His strikeouts soared to 120, the worst in the league.

The following 2 seasons were off-years by Mantle standards. He had over 120 strikeouts each year, and his batting average fell below .300 for the first time since 1953. The old temper problem flared up again.

In 1961 Ralph Houk became the Yankee manager, replacing the retired Casey Stengel. One of Houk's first moves was to appoint Mickey team leader.

The new responsibility helped Mickey handle him-

self better than he had ever done before. The brooding of the previous 2 seasons came to an end. Since Mickey had to set an example for the entire team, he had to control his temper.

Later Mickey praised Houk, saying, "He was the best thing that ever happened to me as a ballplayer."

Mickey's new role was reflected in his performance in 1961. It was the year he and Roger Maris were in a home run contest to break Babe Ruth's season record. Maris finally broke the mark. Mickey, despite the bad knee and the sore

arm, hit 54 homers, his career high. Led by the inspired slugging of these two, the Yankees took their rookie manager to the World Series.

But, once again, the triumph was tarnished by the reappearance of Mickey's World Series jinx. This time it was an abscess, a deep open sore, on his hip. Mickey missed the first 2 games. He could not stand being on the bench for the Series. So, before the third game he had the team doctor stitch the wound closed. The doctor told him it would not work, but Mickey insisted.

In his first time at bat he singled. The run to first tore the stitches out. When Mickey returned to the bench, his pants leg was red with blood.

After the game the abscess had to be treated. Most of the players, stopping in to see how Mickey was, took one look at the ugly wound and left. Tony Kubek stayed to watch. Later he said, "It was awful. You could see the bone. I knew then what kind of guy Mickey was." Mickey still insisted on getting into one more game that Series.

Mickey had his last truly great season in 1961. From then on, the injuries began to cut him down. In 1962 he injured his left knee, the good one. He was out for 30 days. When he returned, he could not take a full cut at the plate. His legs would not support him. Many times after a hard swing, he would fall to his knees, his face contorted with pain.

Yet, despite the pain, Mickey still came through with game-winning hits. He batted .322, second highest in the league, to lead the Yankees to the pennant once more. His courageous performance earned him the MVP.

It was not just what Mickey did at the plate that brought him the award. He led the Yankees by the inspiration of his example.

Elston Howard summed up what Mickey meant to the team. "Mickey's our leader," he said. "When you see how he's had to play, what he's done to play, those legs, now the arms—you've got to be proud of him, proud to play with him. You play harder with him around."

In 1963 Mickey played in only 65 games. First there was a broken bone in his foot, then another injury to his left knee, then yet another knee operation.

The shoulder had gotten so bad by 1965 that Mickey could hardly throw. He had to make all his throws to Tom Tresh, in center, who relayed them to the infield.

Batting had become torture. Mickey told one reporter, "When I swing left-handed, I almost get sick to my stomach." Mickey was no longer capable of batting .300. By the end of the season, he could not swing a bat at all.

That winter an operation on his shoulder gave him a few more seasons. In 1967 Mickey had to become a first baseman. The legs which had once enabled him to make it to first base in 3.1 seconds now made him useless as an outfielder.

Finally, in the spring of 1969 Mickey called it quits. Characteristically, he had thought of the fans first. In his retirement speech he said, "I can't hit when I need to. I can't steal when I want to. I can't score from second when I have to . . . I can no longer deliver what the fans expect of me."

Probably no other athlete had ever gone through so much pain to deliver what the people came to see.

Casey Stengel, thinking of how Mickey had to do it, said, "In the years to come when they read about him in record books, nobody will ever believe that he was a cripple."

And the records he left are incredible: 536 life-time home runs, 3 times MVP, the Triple Crown in 1956, 4 times league home run champion.

While Mickey played for New York, the Yankees won 12 pennants and were World Champions 7 times. Mickey held Series records for most home runs, runs scored, runs batted in, total bases, and extra base hits.

Although people will always talk about what he might have done without the injuries, by any standards Mickey was a great hitter. Yet, he had a certain quality that made him so much more than just another great batsman.

Mickey never seemed to lose the enthusiasm that colored his boyhood dream of baseball stardom. He never really learned to hold himself back—even when he had constant pain to remind him to be careful.

It was his inability to hold back that drove him, as late as 1965, to try to steal 5 bases. He got there 4 times.

And it was that boyish dream of greatness that he carried into games like the one in May, 1963. It was the bottom of the eleventh inning. The air in Yankee Stadium was super-charged with electric excitement as Mickey stepped to the plate. With each pitch the tension became more unbearable.

Then it happened. Mickey unleashed a tremendous swing. There was a crack like an explosion as the ball shot off the bat towards the right field stands, 390 feet away.

Instantly, everyone knew it was gone; and 11 innings of tension exploded into a thunderous, deafening roar. Above the din, the ball, a white blur, just kept soaring higher and higher. It was still going up when it hit the third deck facade which towered some 9 stories above right field. The blast had come within 18 inches of being the first ball ever hit out of Yankee Stadium.

Mickey had done it. He had won the game with his bat, just as he had won so many others. This talent, the ability to come up with big hits at the right times, was what made him a star.

But Mickey was never satisfied with just that. In his desire for greatness, he had to hit the ball harder and farther than anyone had ever hit it before.

In the wonder of what he did that day in May, in the twilight of his career, lies the magic that transformed Mickey Mantle from a star into a legend.

JACK NICKLAUS
BILL RUSSELL
MARK SPITZ
VINCE LOMBARDI
BILLIE JEAN KING
ROBERTO CLEMENTE
JOE NAMATH
BOBBY HULL
HANK AARON
JERRY WEST
TOM SEAVER
JACKIE ROBINSON
MUHAMMAD ALI
O. J. SIMPSON
JOHNNY BENCH
WILT CHAMBERLAIN
ARNOLD PALMER
A. J. FOYT
JOHNNY UNITAS
GORDIE HOWE

# superstars! superstars! superstars!

CREATIVE EDUCATION SPORTS SUPERSTARS

WALT FRAZIER
PHIL AND TONY ESPOSITO
BOB GRIESE
FRANK ROBINSON
PANCHO GONZALES
LEE TREVINO
KAREEM ABDUL JABBAR
JEAN CLAUDE KILLY
EVONNE GOOLAGONG
ARTHUR ASHE
SECRETARIAT
ROGER STAUBACH
FRAN TARKENTON
BOBBY ORR
LARRY CSONKA
BILL WALTON
ALAN PAGE
PEGGY FLEMING
OLGA KORBUT
DON SCHULA
MICKEY MANTLE